Slammin' on the Rails

A Poetry Collection

by

C. D. Melley

Slammin' on the Rails

Slammin' on the Rails
Copyright © 2014 by C. D. Melley

Published by Douglas J. McLeod

Cover Photo: "Ontario Northland FP7 hauled Polar
Bear Express" by Robert Taylor from Stirling,
Canada - Polar Bear Express arrives in Cochrane
from MoosoneeUploaded by Arsenikk. Licensed
under Creative Commons Attribution 2.0 via
Wikimedia Commons -
http://commons.wikimedia.org/wiki/File:Ontario_
Northland_FP7_hauled_Polar_Bear_Express.jpg#
mediaviewer/File:Ontario_Northland_FP7_hauled_
Polar_Bear_Express.jpg

First Paperback Edition: 2014

ISBN: 978-0993773228
ISBN-10: 0993773222

10 9 8 7 6 5 4 3 2 1

To my darling Catherine,
with much love.

Other Books Written by C. D. Melley

The Prairie Fire Within

Insomniac

Just one more cup
Just one more cup
Coffee is my fuel
I am a slave to the bean.

Excitement flows through me when I get my hit
Caffeine is my drug of choice and feeds my adrenaline
There is so much to do and so little time
That's why I turn to the black nectar of the Gods.

I am a disciple to the church of the Double-Double
When I lack it, my body causes trouble
It tires out and I feel useless
And the only thing I can do is what I really need.
Sleep.

H.A.L.T.

Hungry, Angry, Lonely, Tired
The warning signs of when one lets their guard down.

Hunger is the need for sustenance
We crave to be nourished
But when one is in recovery
They must be satisfied in other ways.

Anger is a volatile emotion
That can eat away at the soul
We must calm our frustrations
And use spirituality to become whole.

Loneliness is the emotion
I dread the most
But when surrounded by friends and family
I am never truly alone.

Tiredness is self-explanatory
One can't think when they want to sleep
To make one self-aware
A good night's rest is essential.

Hungry, Angry, Lonely, Tired
The Yield Sign on the Road to Recovery.

My Favourite Feline

Her hair is dark
Like the skies at night
But her eyes sparkle when she looks at me
Stars within the twilight

Her smile lights up the room
And sends my heart a flutter
No woman can do this
She is like no other.

The only regret
Is she is so far away
But, we vowed to be loyal to one another
Our eyes will never go astray.

I dream of her when I sleep
Hoping for that day to come
When I can call her my wife
And together, we will be one.

I know the day is nigh
When we both will walk that aisle
And, our happiness with come alive
We've been waiting a long while.

I love you, my Cat
You mean the world to me
I just hate when we're apart
But together, we shall be.

The Ex from the Forest

She wouldn't admit it
Yet, she enjoyed my company
Her heart was as cold
As the Iced Capps she enjoyed.

I should have known
It wasn't going to last
Her dog wouldn't accept me
That was a definite sign.

She kvetched about her sister
Always being a pain
But, because she couldn't say the words
I was the one who ended up hurt.

Her heart bled blue and white
A rival in my book
For I support the red and black
White and Gold mixed in.

It wasn't going to work from the start
I was blind at first
But, my sight became clear
When she couldn't utter those three words.

Golden Classics

I remember a time
When fire blazed through water
And, walls were mere obstacles
Telling me to change direction.

The visits were cold
Given the time of year
But, a Speedo and swim cap
Were the blankets of my craft.

Horns echo in my memory
Telling me to wake up and smell the chlorine
And, a silent prayer was said
Whenever I flipped in the shallow end.

Metallic trinkets adorned my neck
Symboling my accomplishments
A race well-swam

Two decades have passed
Since I last strapped on my goggles
Yet, I return to this City of Magic
A Golden Spell never forgotten.

Autumn's Wonder

The chill is eminent in the air
The nights grow longer
And the foliage displays
Their kaleidoscope of colour.

The patches are adorned
With gourds filled with orange hue
They remind me of the aroma of nutmeg
For the pies they'll be converted to.

Kids dress in costume
Begging for a haul
Their bellies to be filled
With the sweet treats collected.

And for one special group
Of creative geniuses
Their world gets turned upside-down
In a bid to write for a month.

These are the joys of Fall
My favourite season of all
The harvest is afoot
So, time to have a ball.

Riding the Rails

Watching the scenery go by
On this September morn
I'm amazed by the splendor
This land has to offer.

From small forests to farmland
Trees and corn stalks pass my sight
Little towns dot the landscape
As I look out the train window.

Today is a day for creativity
And, serenity is my companion.
My laptop perched on my thighs
As I type my thoughts today.

The skies overhead are clear
Blueness fills my vista
An odd cloud dots the horizon
The sun rays illuminate the countryside.

There is no better beauty
Than seeing the country by rail
My initial intent was for sport
But, stanzas are today's name of the game.

Yankball

Today is a day
Where North Americans unite
For the calendar reads Sunday
And the juggernauts take the field.

I confess to being a fan
Of the homegrown three-down game
But, when it comes to American sporting culture
Their four-down brand is king.

Some fans plant their tongues in their cheek
When thinking about Detroit, Cincy, and Chitown
Blame Judy Garland
For them saying 'Lions, and Bengals, and Bears. Oh, my!'

Beer is the potent potable of watchers' choice
Nachos and pizza for snacks
They rise to their feet
Everytime a QB gets sacked.

Sunday is for America's Game
And, the gridiron is our church
Our wives will feel lonely this day
And every Lord's Day 'til the parishioners return in February.

The Love Has Risen

She stirs from her slumber
A well-deserved rest
And when she rolls over
The man of her dreams lays beside her.

She leans over to lay a kiss on his cheek
He begins to rouse
His eyes blink open
And sees the vision of beauty smiling at him.

The man grins back at her
And, caresses his darling's face
Knowing out of anywhere in the world
He prefers to be at this place.

The couple greet with a kiss
And, murmur "Good morning"
Then, they curl back up to one another
Not wanting to leave this haven.

They are forced to leave their cocoon
When their dog yips for his food
Another day has begun
And, their love for one another is renewed.

First World Problem

I'd like to file a complaint
Your service is not as advertised
It's supposed to enhance the customer experience
But, it causes headaches for all involved.

How can one get any work done?
Or, check their email?
What about the social media junkies
Who crave their Facebook and Foursquare fix?

You charge us insane prices to begin with
For your fancy spins on a cup of Joe
Although, I cannot resist
The allure of the PSL.

I can understand if it's a bandwidth issue
Too many logging on at once
Or the fact your network is unprotected
Allowing passers-by to tether on.

But, you're supposedly a reputable company
With stores worldwide
But, how do you expect to keep business
When we can't logon to your Wi-Fi?

Fighting the Temptation

Everywhere I turn
People are caught in the vice
Carrying slips of paper
Hoping for the next big win.

The building on the riverfront
With their lights all ablaze
Luring the weak into its clutches
To drain their pockets dry.

It's not easy when you're an addict
The allure is maddening
You try to stay on the straight and narrow
But, the devil keeps dragging you in.

So, what can one do
To combat the insanity?
Follow your spirituality
And your Higher Power will guide you.

That's why I didn't give in
To the foul temptress today
But, I know if I let my guard down for a second
I will be in her clutches again.

Missed Opportunity

I had an option today
To meet a dear friend
An inspiration to my creativity
A sister to my muse.

They were to do a book signing
A first for them
Having the chance to meet their fans
And, peddle the words they've scribed.

However, the sale was out of reach
Not accessible by my means
I could have hiked to meet them
But, my time constraints were limited.

I don't know if I'll get the chance again
To meet my dear friend
A return trip is not on the horizon
In the immediate future.

While I missed my chance
To hook-up with a compatriot
I will still support them, regardless
Alas, it will be from afar.

Crowded Car

The comfort I had on the way down
Was not gifted to me in return
I head back home
Trapped like a sardine.

The rail car is packed
Filled with passengers returning home
This is the last train of the night
And, seating is at a premium.

My legroom is limited
As is my elbow room
The seat ahead is reclined
And I type awkwardly in my perch.

The jigging and reeling of the car
Is a test of my dexterity
Hoping I don't mistype
The stanza du jour.

Three more hours of these cramped quarters
Lord, let them zoom by
For combined with my lack of sleep
My coherence is sketchy.

Thoughts of You

I embarked on this trip
To spark my muse
But, all I have in my head
Are thoughts of you.

I miss holding you in my arms
Your lips upon mine
Telling you how much I love you
Our hearts forever entwined.

I know the day is coming
When we'll be together for life
You can call me your husband
And, I will call you my wife.

But, here I sit on this train
Thinking to myself
My life is empty without you
Your love is its true wealth.

I know our next rendez-vous is uncertain
But, my mind is not in a haze.
I will be with you again
I'm just counting down the days.

Moon Over the Southwest

The sun has almost set
And the moon is full in the sky
My long day is coming to a close
And soon night will take over.

Wolves will bay at the light
And stars will appear
Homeward bound I will continue
My journey is not done yet.

There is still another couple of hours
On this sojourn by rail
The day wasn't like I hoped
But, my muse is satisfied

I will leave this train
To a chill in the air
Autumn is upon us
In a few weeks, the snow will fly.

Regardless, I marvel at the tranquility
As it passes by my window
Southwestern Ontario in its splendor
A vision I'll miss when I leave.

Sleep Come Soon

I don't know why I do this to myself
I get so wrapped up
Excitement gets the better of me
And I pay for it in the end.

I like to think of these all-nighters
As one with the insanity
We do it one weekend every November
In the bid for creativity.

But, this was a solo effort
I have no one else to blame
I wanted to make sure I caught my ride
And, made it I did.

But, it did not come without sacrifice
Walking the streets pre-dawn
Restfulness made way for wakefulness
The former I crave now.

I'll probably collapse on my bed
As soon as I walk through the door.
After the night and day I've had
Sleep will be my reward.